Washington Atlee Burpee

The poultry yard, how to furnish and manage it

Washington Atlee Burpee

The poultry yard, how to furnish and manage it

ISBN/EAN: 9783337147174

Printed in Europe, USA, Canada, Australia, Japan

Cover: Foto ©Lupo / pixelio.de

More available books at **www.hansebooks.com**

HOW TO FURNISH AND MANAGE IT.

A TREATISE FOR THE AMATEUR POULTRY RAISER AND FARMER

ON THE

MANAGEMENT OF POULTRY,

AND THE MERITS OF

THE DIFFERENT BREEDS.

BY

W. ATLEE BURPEE.

AUTHOR OF THE PIGEON LOFT.

PHILADELPHIA, PA.

1877.

PREFACE.

The favorable reception of " The Pigeon Loft ; how to Furnish and Manage it ;" published May, 1875, and the large demand for it, together with numerous inquiries, have induced us to prepare the present treatise on Poultry, in the same form and at the same price. We lay no claims to entire originality in this work. All breeders meet with much the same experience, and it has been our aim to compile from all reliable sources, a concise treatise, at a low price, giving instructions to beginners. We have not attempted an elaborate description of the breeds of poultry, only endeavoring to state their respective merits and demerits, and thus enable every amateur to answer for himself the oft repeated question " which breed pays the best." We would express our indebtedness for valuable hints especially to *The Poultry World*, *The Poultry Nation*, and *Wright's Illustrated Book of Poultry*.

W. A. B.

Philadelphia, March, 1877.

THE POULTRY YARD:

HOW TO FURNISH AND MANAGE IT

Poultry Houses.

Wherever practicable it is preferable to allow fowls entire liberty. Thereby they have abundant muscular exercise, can range at will over wheat stubbles, gathering many a worm, and are kept in the highest degree of health. When thus kept, as is the universal custom of farmers, they must not, however, be allowed to "shift" for themselves, roosting on the trees or wherever they choose. No well-to-do farmer would allow his sheep or pigs to run at random without proper stabling or pens. It is none the less necessary to success in raising fowls that the same attention should be paid to them. It does not pay to constantly clean up the implements, wagons, etc., on which the fowls have passed the night. A farmer cannot afford to lose the droppings of his fowls, as there is no more valuable manure in the world. A thrifty breeder cannot afford the time to hunt over hay mows, under pig pens and amongst the shrubbery for hens' nests—perhaps only to find the eggs when spoiled by incubation. For these and other evident reasons poultry should have a house set apart especially for their wants. They do not require a large or expensive building. A building ten or twelve feet square is large enough for a flock of twenty fowls. The building should be about seven feet in height and should face the south. The roof should be perfectly water proof and the sides free from any cracks or crevices to admit draughts of air. The front, if in a warm climate, can be made of slats, when

abundant ventilation will be allowed. If the winters are
severe it should be entirely closed in front excepting a
small hole for the entrance and exit of fowls and a suitable opening for ventilation at the top. This latter can
be accomplished by simply boring a considerable number
of augur holes near together, or leaving an opening protected by slats arranged after the fashion of Venetian
blinds. A suitable door must of course be made for the
entrance of the keeper. The house must be situated upon
high ground and the floor always dry. Many styles of
poultry houses are in use, and the reader can easily in-
vent one to suit his own taste and surroundings. For
half a dozen fowls a very small house only is necessary.
Unless protected, the entrance hole for the fowls will
admit a great deal of cold air. For the following
simple arrangement we are indebted to the *Poultry
Nation* :—

"Place a box in front of the outlet, tight up against the
side of the house, leaving a hole at either end next the
building. Slanting a board from the ground to the top
of the box in front of the hole, to break the wind in that
direction, you have a house as near wind-proof as though
it were entirely closed. If possible, pile manure, straw,
gravel, or anything you might happen to have handy,
around the box, thus keeping the wind out of the cracks
and making the house warmer."

The interior of the house should be fitted up with
roosts and nests. The roosts should all be on the same
level to prevent fighting for the highest place. They
should not be more than eighteen inches or two feet from
the ground for large fowls, and should be sufficiently
wide. A good plan is to arrange the nests on the floor
under the roosts, protected by a board which will collect
the droppings and which can be readily scraped off.

When we published the "American Fanciers' Gazette," we received a communication on nesting places from an experienced fancier under the *nom de plume* of "Amateur," from which we give the following extract:—

"In almost every plan for the construction of a poultry house an elaborate row of boxes is introduced, cunningly devised with a darkened rear passage, favoring the secresy which mistress Biddy, it is well-known, takes delight in, and who, once ensconced therein, finds everything lovely and serene. But there is one fatal objection to this symmetrical arrangement, according to my experience, which is this—the liability of mistaking the nests and the confusion and loss resulting therefrom.

I have adopted for years the plan of having movable boxes placed on brackets, elevated from one to three feet from the ground. They should be painted in different colors, if possible, so that the hen easily distinguishes her own from others. Nothing could induce me to return to the plan of stationary boxes, as my losses from mistakes have been next to nothing since I adopted this plan of movable nests. A cover of coarse wire netting placed over the sitting hen during the first few days of incubation, will prevent any disturbance afterwards almost certainly."

If the fowls are kept in confinement, or have no other shelter, they should be furnished with a covered run for wet weather. *Cleanliness* is all important, and it is *Foul* management indeed to allow a stench to arise in the fowl house, rendering the very air the fowls breathe impure and creating the presence of the chickens' mortal enemy—vermin. The roosts should be scraped, the droppings removed, and a little fresh ashes, gravel or loam strewn on the floor every morning. Also the nesting material should be changed whenever occasion requires.

The interior of the house, the nests and the perches should all be thoroughly whitewashed every spring and fall. No harbor should be presented for vermin, and the air must always be pure. If fowls are confined in a yard the ground should also be frequently raked and occasionally dug or plowed over.

In constructing the nests, we have already mentioned, it will be well to remember that several hens will frequently lay in the same nest and consequently a smaller number of nests are necessary. Hens should not be set in the roosting and laying house. Some writers recommend a separate house for setting hens, and where poultry are raised in very large numbers this doubtless is desirable, but for the ordinary farmer is entirely unnecessary. The hens can be set on the hay mow, in the barn, wagon-house, an unused stall or any place where they will be quiet and undisturbed.

In breeding several yards of fancy poultry, the usual plan is to make a straight house with yards extending out the entire length and separated by slat fences. This will answer, but is open to the objection that the cocks will occasionally fight through the rails unless the fence is solid at the base, and if ever one slat should fall off woe to the pure breds! A very simple plan for a breeder of several varieties is to give them each a small, separate house and yard situated in different parts of the ground. When the yard space allotted is very small a movable fence can be used, and then the fowls can at any time be transferred to fresh pasturage.

Selection and Mating of Stock.

In selecting fancy stock of course the standard must be followed and only the best and most nearly perfect specimens of their kind retained — *provided they are all suited to each other.* No hen should have the same faults as the cock. If one is faulty in a certain point, the other should be especially good in that particular so as to counteract the bad impress upon the offspring. Experience with each breed must teach the fancier the best birds to retain for breeding. Often a bird that is not up to the standard—and sometimes even a disqualified bird is desirable in the breeding yard, nay, of the highest importance—for instance, in breeding Leghorns a straight comb hen is invaluable to raise the finest and most erect combs on cockerels. So a spotted breasted Dark Brahma and Brown Leghorn cock will produce the most beautiful pencilled pullets. We remember seeing a communication in one of the poultry journals by the late Mr. J. W. P. Hovey, in which he stated the case of a friend who ordered a trio of Brahmas, at a high price, *mated for breeding*, from a celebrated English breeder, and who was disgusted at receiving a poor looking trio of birds whose equals *in looks* could have been purchased anywhere at $2.00 a head! But appearances are deceitful and *blood* will tell, as was proven by the result. From that trio sprung noted prize birds. And so it is, the skillful breeder knows how to mate his birds to produce the best offspring. Amateurs in starting make a great mistake in purchasing exhibition birds (as birds *matched* for exhibition are seldom rightly *mated* for breeding), or in pur-

chasing low priced birds from unknown sources. The
best plan is to send the price of a pair or trio of breeding
birds to a responsible breeder who has a reputa-
tion to maintain, and state plainly that you want
birds whose *progeny* will speak their praises. In nine
cases out of ten you will be satisfied not only in the birds
received but in the chicks they breed. In mating fowls
it is generally believed the hen affects mostly the size
and form, and the cock the plumage and markings of the
chicks. If a choice can be had it is preferred to mate a
cock (over one year old) with spring pullets. Be sure
you select a good vigorous cock and the one who is the
'boss rooster." One cock will readily serve eighteen or
twenty hens of the large breeds and twenty four to thirty
hens of the small breeds

This has been our experience and we first expressed our
views on this subject in an editorial in the "American
Fanciers' Gazette." Instead of meeting the opposition we
might have anticipated from "book fanciers" who had
followed the laws of four to six hens to one cock as laid
down by other authors we received several long letters
giving experience strongly confirming our own. A good
cock with a small number of hens will only worry and
annoy them, often injuring them. With a large number
of hens as stated, some of the hens will of course generally be sitting. This ratio of hens applies to small flocks
of fowls; where the number is multiplied there should be
rather a less proportion of hens, as the majority of the
work will devolve upon the "cocks of the roost." In
selecting the hens those of the greatest utility only should
be used. If layers are desired, prove by actual count
which individual hens lay the most eggs and retain them.
If size and early maturity, select the fowls most nearly
perfect in these respects. Remember that *fat* is preju li-

cial to health and success with breeding fowls. It is not *weight* but a large form—a *capacity* to take on flesh that makes large chicks. See to it that the fowls do not breed large legs and necks—look to the greatest development of the most palatable parts. Raise fowls of bright, yellow skin and legs. These latter remarks are especially intended for the market poulterer, and we will only add that no one can realize the great improvement possible in even " dung-hills " by following up the " survival of the fittest." We cannot make monkeys into men, life is too short for that, but we can vastly improve the condition and value of our poultry. One of our farmers by a source of judicious mating and selecting of mongrel breeding stock so well established a strain of large, well-bred fowls, that he was able to dispose of his surplus stock to dealers at $5.00 a pair. There is no need of the farmer of to day wasting tedious years in the improvement of his barnyard fowls, when for five or ten dollars outlay in the purchase of a cock or pair of pure bred fowls he can avail himself of the labor of others for many years. Poultry should not be bred in-and-in too much, but judicious in-breeding, to a certain extent, is necessary to establish a fixed type or peculiar strain. For ordinary farm use we would recommend the introduction of a thorough bred cock of fresh blood every second year. Farmers cannot realize what a wonderful improvement a thoroughbred cock will make in a flock of mongrel hens. It will not hurt to make one cross of father with daughter, or of son with mother and half-sisters. It is best to kill all hens when two and one-half years old as soon as they begin to moult. After that the supply of eggs falls off greatly and it does not pay to keep them. They can then be sold at a fair compensation. Do not count your chickens before they are hatched is all very true, but none the less will an intelligent breeder

desire *to count his chickens before they die*, and to do this
with profit the breeding stock should be slaughtered for
market at the age already named.

We will conclude our remarks on mating by the following extract, written by us for the " American Fanciers' Gazette," August, 1875 :—

LUCK IN MATING.—So much has been said and written
about *science in breeding*, that we propose, by way of variety, to briefly call the attention of our readers to the
intervention, oftimes, of *luck* in mating. We do not
class ourselves among the believers in mere luck, never-
theless it must be acknowledged that birds mated on the
same system (or oftener perhaps *lack* of system), will and
to produce diverse results. This, when looked at in one
light is not luck, but the rational results of nature's own
laws. However, as far as the breeder is concerned, it is
bound to prove either a *lucky* or an *unlucky match*. For
instance, two birds are selected which are as near ap-
proaches to perfection as the art and skill of the breeder
has attained unto; they are mated, and in some cases the
offspring will be satisfactory, in others (and the chances
are about equal,) they will be most unsatisfactory, the
products coming worthless as mongrels. Now, this can
be explained in some cases by the assumption (if the birds
were of different but unknown strains,) that the strains of
which they are members had been bred for different
results, and the one still possessed the fault which had
just been eradicated from the other but of which a tendency remained. Then these two birds possessing an
inherent inclination to like faults, the offspring come
possessed of those faults to a double degree. Again, the
strains being bred for diverse purposes, all the breeder's
pains are crushed to the ground by this sudden union, and
nature will advocate its power. Now on the other hand

if these birds are differently mated, they may *luckily* be paired to suitable birds, and then become the progenitors of worthy offspring.

All that we have just now said shows that there is at bottom, in such cases, although the breeder may be ignorant thereof, a natural cause for these *lucky* or *unlucky* results. That such, beyond doubt, is the fact, in nine cases out of ten of the varied results of promiscuous matings we are ready to acknowledge. But, on the other hand, the experienced breeder has, or doubtless will come across cases which can be explained upon no such ground. Despite all his care and *system* in breeding and mating, results (we do not mean an occasional exceptional bird, but *regularly*) contrary to the skilled breeder's expectations, will crop out. And then, when the same birds are mated to other birds of the *same blood* as the previous matings, and having like defects and " fine points," vastly different will be the results. Not only so, but we have known different cases of two birds upon being mated together proving entirely sterile and unfertile, while both of these birds being put to different mates were perfectly capable of reproducing sound and healthy offspring. We could particularize cases which might more vividly illustrate the point at issue, but as we have already consumed considerable space, we do not think it necessary, as we can vouch for the truth of the above statements.

What and How to Feed.

It is the general habit of Americans to give their poultry corn, corn, corn, morning, noon and night. This may answer when the fowls have the unlimited range of a farm and can constantly pick up insects, grubs, worms, etc., together with scattered grains around the barn floor, but even then it is very inadvisable. In confinement fowls would soon die on this diet. Corn is too heating and fattening for breeding purposes. Fowls should be fed *regularly.* They will soon learn the accustomed hours and will employ the intervening time in hunting for worms, dusting and exercising themselves. Where they are at liberty or have a large run, two feeds a day, morning and evening, are sufficient. It is best to make the morning meal of soft food, that being most readily assimilated will the sooner appease their empty stomachs and break the fast of the night. Boiled potato peelings, vegetables and scraps mashed up with slightly scalded bran or meal with a little salt mixed, is an excellent dish for fowls. In winter a little pepper will be valuable as a seasoning.

As a soft food the *Poultry World* recommends a warm compound of two-thirds wheat bran to one-third meal, wet with skimmed milk. This food has a good egg producing effect. The bran does not tend to fat and the milk is even better than meat in the production of eggs. Fowls may eat too much meat, but milk they may drink *ad libitum,* and those who have it cannot put it to a more profitable use. Fowls should have, like human beings, a goodly *variety* of feed. Scraps from the table are highly relished. Grain should be fed at night as it will remain in their crops longest. Corn is the best staple feed for cold weather, as it is very heating and keeps the fowls in fine condition, but it should not be fed constantly in summer. Barley, buckwheat, oats, wheat screenings, cracked corn, rice, etc., are all excellent for a variety. Sunflower seed is invaluable for poultry and can be grown as cheaply as corn. The Mammoth Russian is the best and most prolific. Single heads which we raised this year will measure one foot in diameter and are well filled with an immense number of large plump seeds. Breeding fowls must not be over fed nor stuffed but only kept in good working order. Beef scraps can be bought cheap, and are highly beneficial, in winter especially, also occasionally a boiled sheep's or calf's pluck chopped up is recommended In concluding our remarks on the feed of fowls we cannot do better than append Lewis Wright's valuable table of the respective constituents of the various grains, etc, generally used for poultry, from which intelligent poulterers can draw their own conclusions:—

TABLE

There is in every 100 parts by weight of	Flesh-forming Materials Gluten, &c	Warmth giving and Fattening Material, viz		Bone-making Materials, or Mineral Substances.	Husk or Fibre.	Water.
		Fat or Oil.	Starch.			
Beans & Peas.	25	2	48	2	8	15
Oatmeal	18	6	63	2	2	9
Middlings Thirds or fine Sharps.	18	6	53	5	4	14
Oats	15	6	47	2	20	10
Wheat	12	3	70	2	1	12
Buckwheat	12	6	58	1½	11	11½
Barley	11	2	60	2	14	11
Indian Corn	11	8	65	1	5	10
Hempseed	10	21	45	2	14	8
Rice	7	A trace.	80	A trace.	...	13
Potatoes	6½	—	41	2	...	50½
Milk	4½	3	5	¾	...	86¾

On most farms both fowls and ducks are allowed to run together, hence it is sometimes desirable to feed the one and not the other. The "American Agriculturist" suggests the following ingenious plan :—

"The fowls can be readily fed by putting the feed on boards slightly elevated from the ground : the ducks seldom attempt to fly up. To feed the ducks and not the fowls, a large flat pan should be procured and several bricks placed in the middle in order to keep the food around the edges. Then a large inverted box or tub should be covered over the pan, supported by a brick in each corner. The ducks by the flexibility of their necks are enabled to feed, while the fowls can get nothing."

Fowls require a constant supply of pure fresh water. It is well occasionally to add a few drops of sulphate of iron to the water. The indestructible stone drinking fountains so generally used are well adapted to hold the supply. A large one on the same principle can easily be made out of any old keg or small barrel. Insert a spicket near the bottom and let its mouth rest in a movable tin cup—the water will flow out only so fast as it is consumed in the cup. A cover should be prepared for the tin in order to prevent the birds from fouling the water. This is best done by an oblong frame to fit over the cup, —solid light wood at the sides and slanting top,—the front being made of perpendicular wires. The water should be changed at least once or twice a day on excessively warm days in summer. In winter, once in three or four days is amply sufficient. It may often be desirable to give the feed in a hopper, when we would recommend one of the pattern described in "The Pigeon Loft." We would here state that buttermilk and curds are highly relished by the fowls and are very nutritious.

It now behooves us to mention the condiments requisite to good health in our feathered pets. These are neither many nor expensive, but are all important to the thrift and well being of fowls. Poultry must have *lime* in some form for the formation of egg shell. Crushed oyster shells are the most desirable. They can be procured at a low price, crushed finely by machinery, at any dealer's store. Old mortar will also answer. They must have access to plenty of gravel containing small stones which are a necessary aid to digestion. These are the "hen's teeth." Granulated or pure ground bone is invaluable for poultry and it can be fed either in a dish or hopper or scattered on the ground like corn. Broken charcoal should be supplied. It abundantly stimulates digestion and also acts as a purifier in cases of Roup, etc.

Fowls in confinement must have plenty of dust in which to cleanse themselves. Road dust is the best. Coal ashes are also good for this purpose. Customers have often asked our opinion as to the value of prepared food advertised for poultry. These preparations are as a rule tonics which stimulate the production of eggs in fowls. From the great demand for the "Imperial Egg Food," (at present the leading preparation of its kind), we know it is generally satisfactory. There is no doubt that the production of eggs is increased thereby, and it is a good thing for fowls, especially when kept in confinement. But it must always be remembered that *breeding* fowls should be in a *natural* condition—never overfed or too much forced by stimulants.

General Management.

Success in any branch of business or industry is achieved only by the most diligent and the most eager to improve every opportunity. We often receive letters from men whose health has failed, very frequently disabled ministers, who desire some easy occupation whereby they can gain an honest livelihood and who are inclined to favor poultry breeding. A man is always safe to keep out of a business he knows nothing about. If, however, a good opening presents itself, we can safely say the raising of first-class poultry can be soon learned. We would advise new beginners to start on a small scale and gradually increase. Poultry costs less to produce than beef, and brings a higher average price. Fowls and eggs are always in demand. The intelligent poulterer can often secure a slight advance on the ordinary market rates by invariably selling a superior article to appreciative customers. To succeed in the poultry business, one should have a natural love for fowls and should start determined to devote to the breeding of fowls the same application and study which would be necessary to success in any business undertaking. Conducted on business principles, poultry breeding is as profitable—considering the small amount of capital required—as any of the lines of trade, and is not nearly so much overdone. But especially to the general farmer is poultry breeding remunerative. Fowls pay a speedy return for the money expended, and no farm stock yields a larger per centage on the capital invested. In breeding fowls there is one quite important item that is often neglected. We allude to the value of

poultry manure.   Wright states that he found that droppings from four Brahmas, for one night, weighed, in one
case, exactly one pound ; and in another more than three-
quarters. an average of nearly four ounces each bird.
By drying, this was reduced to 1½ ounces.   Other breeds
make less ; but allowing only 1 ounce per bird daily, of
dry dung, fifty fowls will make in their roosting-house
alone, about 10 cwt. per annum of the best manure in
the world.   Hence, in half a year this number of fowls,
to say nothing of their offspring, will make more than
enough manure for an acre of land, 7 cwt. of guano being
the usual quantity applied per acre, and poultry manure
being even richer than guano in ammonia and fertilizing
salts.   These figures demand careful attention from the
large farmer.   The manure, before using, should be mixed
with twice its bulk of earth, and then allowed to stand
in a heap covered with a few inches of earth, till decom-
posed throughout, when it makes the very best manure
that can be had.

We quote this to show that no "little things," which
seem but trifling economies, should be neglected, but
everything possible should be made a source of revenue.
The droppings must be kept dry, under cover.   If fowls
are slaughtered in large quantities the feathers also will
be worth saving.   The webs of the large feathers should
be stripped from the quills and the smaller ones left as
they are.   They should be cured by baking four times in
a cool oven, about half an hour each time, and allowed to
dry for a couple of days between each baking.   In supplying the market it is very desirable to have winter
eggs.   A little foresight will secure a good supply.   Animal food must be furnished.

Dressing and Shipping Poultry.

On this subject we quote the following as given by a large commission house ;

"In preparing poultry for market, do not feed for at least twenty-four hours before killing, as food in the crop injures the appearance, is liable to sour, and purchasers object to paying for this worse than useless weight. Opening the veins of the neck is the best mode of killing, and let it bleed freely, as poultry not properly bled will not have a bright healthy appearance. The intestines or the crop should not be "drawn." For scalding poultry, the water should be as near to the boiling point as possible, without actually boiling ; the bird being held by the head and legs, should be immersed and lifted up and down in the water three times—this makes picking easy. When the head is immersed it turns the color of the comb, and gives the eyes a shrunken appearance, which often leads buyers to think the fowl has been sick. The feathers should then be at once removed, pin feathers and all, very cleanly, and without breaking the skin. It should next be "plumped," by being dipped about ten seconds into water, nearly or quite boiling hot, and then once into cold water about the same length of time. Most of the dressed poultry sold here is wet-picked, and such is generally preferred; but very fat, handsome turkeys, dry-picked, sell well at Thanksgiving and Christmas. Great care should be taken to avoid cutting or bruising the flesh or breaking the bones. It should be entirely cold, but not frozen before being packed. This is a matter of importance; for if packed with the animal heat in it, it will be almost sure to spoil. If it reaches market sound, without freezing, it will sell all the better. In packing, when practicable, use hand-threshed dry straw; be sure that it is clean, free from dust of any kind, and entirely dry. Place a layer of straw at the bottom, then alternate layers of poultry and straw, taking care to stow snugly, backs upward, legs not doubled up under the body, but straightened out, and fill the package so that the cover will draw down very snugly upon the contents, to prevent shifting or shucking on the way. Boxes are the best packages, and should contain from 100 to 200 pounds. Larger boxes are inconvenient, and more apt to get injured The objection to barrels is, that the poultry is apt to be much bent and twisted out of shape; they answer better for chickens and ducks than for turkeys and geese; but when packed in barrels, should be packed on the side, keeping the legs out straight. Straw should be between the poultry and sides of package to keep from freezing, though in very cold weather this cannot always be avoided. In packing large lots, avoid putting more than one kind in a package and mark the kind on the cover.

In preparing frozen poultry for the late market, dry pick the poultry, as it will keep longer, hold its color better, and command better prices; the head should be left on, and the manner of packing much the same as in the general directions, except no straw or packing of any kind should be used. Boxes of the following dimensions are preferable—say four feet long by two feet wide and fifteen inches deep (outside measurement.) Use new inch lumber, well seasoned, and smoothly planed for the inside of the package; they will pack two layers of turkeys or three of fowl. Larger sized packages are inconvenient to handle, and do not meet with as ready a sale; pack a layer of poultry in as many boxes as will be required to mkae one layer for each day's work; when frozen suffi-

ciently, the second layer may be packed in like manner:
when full, the covers should be placed on and snugly
nailed, and the boxes placed together and well covered
with straw—say two or three feet in depth, or should the
weather moisten and thaw when the boxes are but partly
filled, they should be protected in the same way, in
which manner the poultry can be held and forwarded
with entire safety. The packing should be done in a
cold, dry room, separate from the slaughter-house, and
not in the open air, as the wind is apt to turn the poultry dark. Mark plainly on each package the gross
weight and tare, and the kind it contains."

EGGS & CHICKS.

Eggs should be regularly collected every day. The
wide-awake fancier can often learn to distinguish the
eggs of individual hens, and when this is possible it is
very desirable. Thereby, when it is desired to set a hen,
the eggs can be retained only from the finest hens or
those that are the best layers. Hens of the laying breed
will lay 150 to 250 eggs per annum—common hens average about 100 eggs per head. Every nest must always
have a nest egg (white china is the best,) as it prevents
the hens from laying away. Hard shell eggs are always
preferable, and hence it must be seen to that the hens
have constant access to shell-forming material. It is not
best to give them this in the form of broken eggshells, as
they may from that acquire the unprofitable habit of
eating their own eggs. The cure recommended, if the
habit is detected early, is to place in the nest an eggshell
filled with the strongest mustard mixed rather thick.

We often have inquiries as to whether eggs for hatching can be sent safely by express for long distances. We answer unhesitatingly, Yes! We have sent eggs hundreds of miles by express and had 11 and 13 to hatch out of a clutch (13.) And again, we have sent eggs equally as far and *had none to hatch*. Then the purchaser, if he is a novice, is apt to think himself swindled and write a very ungentlemanly letter. There is of course always some risk in transportation, but there are many other reasons why the eggs will sometimes fail to hatch whether sent by express or set at home. Our plan for shipping eggs for hatching is to take a good sized box and make a "cushion" on the bottom *inside* with hay one or two inches deep, then spread a layer of bran, on which pack the eggs, each nearly one inch apart and the same distance from the sides of the box. Cover with bran and then fill up with a good layer of hay. In cold weather each egg should be neatly wrapped in a piece of paper. The lid of the box should be gently *screwed* on. The box should have a handle of a piece of leather or the rim of a barrel. When eggs are ordered from a distance a sitting hen should be in readiness to receive them as soon as they arrive. If none of the hens are ready a broody hen can always be bought at a low figure from some neighboring farmer or "swapped" for a laying hen. To make the hen take to her new nest she should be changed at night, and it should be as nearly as possible like her old nest. She should first be given some china eggs until she settles down quietly to incubation. The period of incubation is twenty-one days. Right here we might say that to preserve eggs for family use the best plan recommended in "Wright's Book of Poultry," is to pack them closely together and keep tightly covered up in a mixture prepared as follows:—

"To four gallons of boiling water, half a peck of new lime, stirring it some little time. When cold, remove any hard lumps by a coarse sieve, add ten ounces of salt and three ounces of cream of tartar and mix the whole strongly. The mixture is then to be let stand to temper for a fortnight before use. Thus treated, if put in when newly laid, at nine months after they will eat quite as good as though only laid six days, though, of course, not quite like *new* laid."

In keeping fowls for eggs it is not necessary or even desirable to have a cock with the hens. Virgin eggs are preferred by epicures and will sometimes bring a slight advance in price on that account. To raise fowls in large numbers they should be colonized in separate families. Twenty five or thirty breeding fowls are plenty in one flock. An experienced poulterer once remarked to us that he could raise more young chicks and make more money from a flock of twenty-five fowls on his farm than he could from fifty—and we believe him. If it is desired to raise poultry in large numbers they should have separate yards, with plenty of room. When this plan is adopted and at the same time eggs are the desired product, one pen of the finest fowls can be mated to replenish the stock and in the others no cocks will be necessary. In breeding fowls in separate enclosures in this manner it will be well to allow each flock on different days in rotation the range of the farm. When fancy fowls are bred it is always well to keep a sufficient number of common hens as sitters. Do not confine your fowls in too close quarters. We constantly see the bad effects of this misman agement. The fowls become enfeebled, lose their vital powers and, as a consequence, the eggs are often worth less. Whenever it is practicable, we advocate unlimited range. When fowls are bred in confinement their wants

must be constantly kept in view and a plentiful supply
of some greens, scraps, worms, etc. given. Some large
breeders of thoroughbred poultry now adopt the plan of
"farming out" their breeding stock. This has always
been our plan, and it has worked very well. We now
employ about thirty different farms in raising pure-bred
poultry for us. We furnish the breeding-stock (to responsible parties only, in the neighborhood,) and pay
a specified price per dozen for eggs and per pair for the
chicks that are fit to sell. The inferior chicks are marketed and the farmer pockets the proceeds. Every year
we mate our breeding stock ourselves for the season. In
putting our fowls out this way we are careful to give each
farmer a breed he *fancies*. We make it to his best inter-
ests to serve us well, by paying him better than he could
do with his own poultry.

Hens should be set in the evening and should be furnished with comfortable nests in a darkened and unmo-
lested spot. The nest should be made flat, (when very
concave the eggs do no not lay so well), and is best
made out of an inverted sod, or three layers of dry
earth or ashes with straw, hay, or forest leaves
placed thereon. Thirteen eggs are the best number covered by average hens. But in cold weather eleven or
even nine or seven—according to the size of the hens
and eggs—are amply sufficient. A larger number would
only become chilled. The hen should be taken off the
nest, (if she does not go off of her own accord) every day
for feed, water, brief exercise and a good dusting. Do
not, as a rule, remove the young chickens until twenty-
four hours after all are hatched. Occasionally one may
need some assistance to get from the shell. This should
be given cautiously, and only in extreme cases, by gently
indenting the finger into the shell (without touching the

inside membrane,) in a circle from where it is clipped.
When the chicks are hatched the mother should be
placed in a coop about two or three feet square, placed on
the ground and with slats in the front, through which
the chicks can run out to exercise and receive feed
Young chicks should always be kept dry and where they
can get plenty of sunlight. It must be remembered that
fowls attain their growth in from four to eight months,
and can never make up for any "back setts" in that
period. Feed regularly and often until five or six weeks
old, at first with cooked meal and hard boiled eggs
mixed. Give fine chopped green feed and let them have
the benefit of a grass run. The floor of the chicken coop
should always be kept clean and free from vermin by a
fresh supply of dry dirt. Chicks should always be kept
growing while young. If intended for marketing they
should be forced and marketed early—Spring chickens
pay the best by all odds. For breeders, however, it is
not necessary to hatch the chicks too early, as those
hatched in milder weather require less care, grow better,
and are fully as profitable. Asiatics, however, intended
for for fall shows, should be hatched by the first of
March. April, May and June, however, are the best
months for hatching fowls intended for breeders. After
the first few days a small bit of meat can be chopped
with the feed once a day. Soft feed should be fed fresh very
often—only so much given each time as is entirely consumed. A little bone meal should be added to the feed.
After the chicks are two or three weeks old, the evening
meal can consist of cracked corn and wheat or good
screenings. Chicks should always have a grass run; if
deprived of this, green feed must be furnished to them
daily. Chopped cabbage leaves are highly relished by
them. A plentiful supply of pure fresh water must be

constantly at hand. In winter the chicks require more stimulating food than in summer. Beef scraps can be boiled and mixed with the soft feed. If the chicks have been liberally fed they will be in prime condition for the table without any extra fattening. Growing chicks must always have plenty of exercise and should not be crowded together in too close quarters. In raising fowls for market, as a rule, the chicks should be killed as soon as ready. Certainly as soon as they have attained full size, as then better prices are generally procured than later in the season. The feed afterwards fed is therefore worse than wasted. Besides this there is considerable risk from disease in holding a large lot of poultry. In breeding fancy fowls the young chicks that turn out inferior "culls" or "scrubs" as commonly called (and alas! even the best strains will sometimes throw these despised and ought-to-be rejected specimens), should be marketed as soon as distinguishable at from three to six months old. Don't be afraid to kill your poor chicks—it is the only way to ultimate success. If all are killed this year they will be fewer next year.

DISEASES.

We do not much believe in doctoring fowls. In fact we have had very little disease amongst our fowls and when it did appear we generally resorted to the hatchet. If we can't cure we can at least kill and thereby prevent the spread of the disease. Prevention is always better than cure. VERMIN are a very frequent cause of disease in fowls. Every precaution should be taken to prevent their appearance. Don't *crowd* the fowls, or—as the

Poultry World tersely remarks—you will breed thousands
of vermin and precious few chicks. The poultry house
should be thoroughly whitewashed inside and out, in the
nests and every crevice, three or four times a year. Mix
2 oz. of carbolic acid to a bucketfull of hot whitewash.
The house should occasionally be fumigated with sulphur.
The nests should be strewn with tobacco dust and sulphur.
The ground powder of the leaves of an imported
plant known in commerce as *Persian Powder*, and
various other names, is the most powerful exterminator
of insects. The odor kills them. The feathers of the
hens should be thoroughly rubbed with the powder.
Gapes will seldom appear in young chicks if the hen and
nests are thoroughly rid of all insects.

Roup, including colds, canker, diphtheria, etc., is best
prevented and often cured by the use of the celebrated
Douglass mixture. This consists of

$\frac{1}{2}$ pound Sulphate of Iron ;

1 oz. Sulphuric Acid ;

2 Gallons Water.

This is to be added to the drinking water in the proportion of a tablespoonful to a pint. Fowls affected by the
Roup should be separated and put in dry warm quarters.
The head and nostrils should be well washed with warm
water and also with warm alum water. Give daily half a
grain Cayenne pepper with half a grain allspice in a bolus
of meal. GAPES, if treated early, a small pill of camphor
daily, and also a little camphor in the drinking water, is
recommended. When fully developed the worms should
be removed from the windpipe by inserting a loop of
horse hair into the organ and withdrawing it while turn-
ing it around. Repeat the operation until all the worms
are removed.

For GENERAL DEBILITY, bad moulting, etc., use stimulating food, with sulphate of iron or Douglass mixture in
the water. If the fowls are in general affected with
disease, especially in the case of Catarrh and Roup, it is
an excellent plan to thoroughly fumigate the poultry
house with sulphur. To do this, close the doors and
windows and burn a small quantity on a shovel. In
many such cases the following prescription will be found
valuable. It was given to us by a doctor fancier some
two years ago, who recommends it as very successful in
most cases of disease among the chickens:—

Pulv. Capsicum, } Ea. 50 grains.
Do.   Allspice,   }

Diluted Carbolic Acid, 2 scruples;

To form into a mass, add Syrup and Flour or powdered
Gum Arabic.

To form into pills 100 of $\frac{1}{2}$ gr. each.

One pill three times a day, or alternate with boluses, as
below:

Pulv. Charcoal and Yeast, 200 grs.

Flor Sulphur, 150 grs.

Syrup of flour, 2 scruples.

To form into mass, which make into 100 boluses of $5\frac{1}{2}$
grs. each.

One 3 times a day.

With Roup give also 3 or 4 drops diluted Carbolic
Acid, washing out nostrils with Castile water, and inject
some of the acid into the nose.

CROP BOUND. The following is recommended:—

Warm water should be forced down the throat and
the crop gently kneaded or worked for an hour, if necessary, until it becomes soft, holding the bill open and the
head down; then give a tablespoonful of castor oil and
feed sparingly for a day or two to prevent permanent dis-

tention.   If this is not effective an incision about an inch
long should be made at the top of the crop, first remo-
ving some of the feathers, and care being taken not to
cut any of the large blood vessels.   The contents of the
crop should then be removed and the outlet examined to
see that it is not stopped up.   The incision may be
closed by making three or four stitches with horse hair
or silk in the inner skin and the same in the outer.   Be
careful not to sew the two skins together, as it is almost
certainly fatal.   Feed on sopped bread, and allow no
water for twenty-four hours after the operation.

STRAINED HIP JOINT.—A customer of ours, and for
many years a practical breeder, has called our attention
to a common ailment in fowls which we believe has
never before been noticed by any writer on poultry.
Especially in the large breeds where the rooster is heavy,
good laying hens after two years old often become so
strained and weak in the hip joints that they slide out
of position, letting the body fall very near the ground
and making the hen walk like a duck.   The rooster
seeing the hen in this position naturally thinks she is
courting his attentions, and the weakened hen is thus
very much injured.   The remedy is simple and the cure
nearly always complete.   Tie the two legs together by a
string around each at the hip joints—a little nearer than
they would be when the bird was standing naturally.
They must be tied back of the breastbone, so that they
cannot slip out of position.   The hen will soon learn to
walk, although not so rapidly, using her hock joints, and
in a few weeks she will have recovered the full and perfect use of her limbs.

How to Raise Good Turkeys.

No farm stock pays higher or surer return for the capital and time invested than turkeys, yet they are often very poorly managed and the profits are consequently meagre. We are convinced this neglect is frequently due to want of a proper knowledge of how to breed and manage them, and hence we shall give full and explicit directions on this subject. Turkey hens attain ma. turity much earlier than the gobblers. At two years old the hens will be full grown; they very seldom become larger after that time; whilst gobblers are not nearly matured at that age, but continue to grow until four or five years old. They are, however, in their prime breeding condition at three years old. Gobblers of this age mated to hens two years old will produce the finest, largest and earliest matured young turkeys. The only objection to gobblers of this age is, that on account of their heavy size they will sometimes injure the hens. For this reason the gobblers although of *large frame* should not be allowed to lay on fat and become heavy during the breeding season.

As a necessary preventive of injury to the hens the spurs and toe nails of the gobbler should be cut off. After the operation the best and most speedy way to stop the bleeding is to saturate a rag with *Monsell's Liquid Solution of Iron*, (which can be procured from any druggist,) and tie over the bleeding parts for a day or two. It will immediately stop the blood. A yearling gobbler of large size mated to two year old hens will also produce fine and large offspring. Great care must always be taken in the selection of the breeding birds. It is very "penny wise and pound foolish" to slaughter and market the largest young turkeys because they will bring a few more cents in market. Those that grow the fastest and largest and are of the most perfect form should not be sold at any price but should be retained for breeders. In a few years the increase in the average size and value of the flock will be so apparent as to convince the farmer that this is beyond all doubt the only right way and by far the most profitable. We cannot too strongly urge this upon our readers. Turkeys are as sure of being improved or degenerated by the manner in which they are bred and selected as are pigs. It will pay every one who raises turkeys to pay eight or ten dollars for a good thoroughbred gobbler to breed from. The gobbler should not be akin to the hens. In selecting birds for breeding, care must be taken that they possess no deformities. Crooked breast, which means what meat there is, all developed on one side of the breast or bone, is often caused by narrow roosting perches. A rail split in half makes an excellent roost. The roosts should not be too high, if in a house, as the turkeys not having room to take a long fly in descending are often seriously hurt. The roosts need not be all on the same level, but can slant in the form of gradually ascending steps. The largest and heaviest old gobblers will often prefer the lowest roost It is useless to attempt to keep turkeys in the same house with hens. While they will generally thrive well roosting out in the trees, &c., yet, for evident reasons, it is always best to have a special house for them. This need only be a shed facing the south and open in front: roo sloping from about nine to seven feet. Turkeys must have liberty and freedom to range at will. They will then pick up much of their feed, but should always be fed regularly every morning and evening. They will then always roost around home and will be kept constantly in fine growing condition. Mr. Thos. Y. England informs us that by actual experiment he has found that if the soft feed (such as meal, etc.) be mixed with *milk* instead of water, the turkeys when killed will be much more delicate and the flesh of a far superior quality to those fed on a mixture made with water. Cottage cheese is an excellent mess for them. Among other valuable hints he also calls attention to the fact that turkey hens after three years old are unprofitable as breeders, often laying soft shelled eggs. The same thing will happen if the turkey hens have not been set during the season. A turkey will lay eighteen or twenty eggs. The eggs of the first laying can be given to hens and the second laying will then be had earlier, when she should be allowed to sit herself, but should be given only so many eggs as she will cover satisfactorily. They begin to lay about April, and unless closely watched will make their nest in the field or among the shrubbery where their eggs may be lost. If a hen is discovered in some such place after she has begun to set it will be well to afford all the protection possible by placing a cover or inverted box, with one side out, over the nest. The period of incubation is twenty-eight days.

It is an undoubted fact that one impregnation of the gobbler fecundates the entire laying of the turkey hen, and yet it is advisable to keep the gobbler constantly with the hens.

Turkey hens are persistent sitters; they frequently have to be compelled to leave the nest for food and water

The French, who are always such studious economists, avail themselves of this propensity to a very good profit in the hatching of chicks. A turkey hen will sit steadily for three months. By giving a little brandy the hen will sit still longer. One great merit is, that they will during all this while keep in such good condition, that they can easily be fattened and killed when their services are no longer needed. Turkeys are very tender when young—until they finish "shooting the red." When the eggs are all hatched the hen turkeys should be confined in a small coop placed in an enclosure of about six feet square, surrounded by a board twelve or fifteen inches high. After awhile the hen can be allowed her freedom. She will guard her chicks carefully and will stay in the enclosure with them or near by. The young Turkeys must not be subjected to dampness nor allowed to run in wet grass. When about three weeks old they can be allowed their liberty with the hen on fine days. They must be fed "little and often" and allowed to get no "back sets." At first feed bread thoroughly soaked in milk and give new milk to drink. Give hard boiled eggs mashed up and mixed with the bread and milk. Feed at least four or five times a day, giving each time just so much as they eat up clean. After a week or two give them curds and continue until five or six weeks old. At this age feed scalded Indian meal mixed with curd: also at another time in the day give scalded Indian, wheat midlings and bran mixed, the mixture to be ⅔ bran. Turkeys must be liberally fed and after they are safe through the critical period of their lives will gain in size very rapidly. They should be fed on stimulating food during moulting season on account of the great rapidity of shedding and the wonderful change they then undergo. From being stark naked they will be entirely feathered in a few weeks.

They are at this time, of course, lighter in weight. A curious fact and one worthy of notice, is that the hens will not moult until they are through sitting. Hence if from any cause they are set very late the moulting is correspondingly later. We have known a hen to be entirely bare at Christmas. This must by all means be avoided, or the hens will likely not be able to withstand the trying ordeal. It has been observed that turkeys show a great fondness for dandelion leaves, in preference to all other greens. From the well-known medicinal properties of this plant, it will be well to sow a few seeds in some waste spot near the turkey house, so that they can have a constant supply.

VARIETIES of Turkeys, are the Mammoth Bronze, White Holland, Black, Blue and Buff Turkeys. The BRONZE TURKEYS are generally considered the largest. Adult gobblers will weigh 40 and 45 pounds each, hens 15 to 20. Young Turkey Gobblers at eight months old, will weigh from twenty-two to twenty-five pounds each and hens from thirteen to fifteen pounds. These are fair average weights. They will gain about one pound in two weeks. But occasionally, and also when birds are especially well fed, they will exceed these weights. For breeding stock, however, it is not well to force them too much. Further north where the snow is on the ground for a longer period and where consequently the Turkeys are fed more corn, they will weigh heavier. The new American standard only recognizes the light tipped turkeys, while the dark bronze are really the more beautiful and by many breeders preferred. Both colors can be bred from the same flock if they are so mated, but some of this offspring will be of a mixed bronze plumage. The silver tips, however, are generally purer bred. The dark bronze will often throw buff or cinnamon birds, showing that they have been crossed with that variety to secure the desired color. Pure bronze turkeys are believed to have originated from a cross of the wild turkey and the grey Narragansetts.

THE WHITE HOLLAND TURKEYS are a very handsome and showy variety. The rich red beads and the intense glossy black beard of the male contrasting beautifully with a plumage of snowy whiteness. For a lawn a finer or more aristocratic ornament could not be desired. They are not only "a thing of beauty," but are also a very valuable breed. They are very much larger than the common white turkey, and also, unlike them, are very hardy. Their flesh is much esteemed as of a superior delicacy. They are especially valued on account of their superior laying qualities and early mating. While their eggs are not quite as large as the bronze, they furnish more of them.

BLACK TURKEYS are distinguished by an intense deep black color throughout, and are of large size.

BLUE TURKEYS, sometimes called slate turkeys, should be of an even slaty color throughout. The best stock of this breed was imported from France. They are much esteemed on account of their prolificacy, early maturity and large size, being in many cases fully equal in size to the Bronze. This breed is well worthy of more general cultivation.

BUFF TURKEYS are as their name indicates, of a pure buff color throughout. They are comparatively but little bred. In no stock is the importance of a good male so fully evinced, and every farmer should each year or two, as already hinted, procure a good thoroughbred gobbler of either the Bronze, White, Holland, or Blue varieties.

RAISING GEESE.

No land or water fowls can be so easily and cheaply raised as Geese. They will thrive well on pasture alone. It is of the first importance to breed from large matured specimens, and when once mated, the same birds can be retained as breeders for very many years. The gander, however, is apt to get cross with age, and hence has to be changed. Two or three geese (or sometimes four) can be mated to one gander. The goose will lay 13 to 15 eggs. When ready for setting, she should have only 13 eggs. She is a splendid sitter, and should not be disturbed. When leaving the nest to feed she covers her eggs like the duck, although not so well. The period of incubation is thirty days. They usually commence laying in February. Large common hens, Cochins or Brahmas can be used as sitters, giving each hen three or four eggs. Turkeys will also hatch the eggs well. On account of the thick shells of the eggs and the long period of incubation, it is recommended to make the nest on the ground or moist earth, and during the last ten days or two weeks to sprinkle the eggs with tepid water. The gander will frequently assist his favorite mate in the labors of incubation, and after the goslings are hatched is very vigilant in his care of them. At first the goslings should be kept warm and fed " little and often," with hard boiled eggs, bread crumbs or scalded meal, not neglecting a plentiful supply of greens and grass. They are soon ready to turn out to graze, and will pick all their food, mostly grass, in the fields. They require no other feed so long as this lasts, and they can be marketed in fine condition, called

in England "green geese." After the supply of grass is
cut off by winter, the geese can be put up to fatten, if so
desired. This should be done in a dark place, and they
should be well fed, on oats, meal or barley meal, or a
mixture. A bunch of sweet hay should be tied up within
their reach.

Geese can be raised profitably with very little water,
only plenty to drink and a large tub full for bathing.
One valuable peculiarity of geese is that they always give
notice of hen-roost robbers, whether biped or quadruped,
by their shrill cries, and hence are excellent "watch
dogs."

THE VARIETIES OF THOROUGHBRED GEESE are the Toulouse, Embden and China. The value of thoroughbreds
is here fully illustrated. For while the produce of pure
Embden geese, crossed with a Toulouse Gander, make the
very finest and largest goslings for the market, yet these,
if bred together, will rapidly deteriorate.

THE TOULOUSE GEESE are of an even shade of grey,
with white on the belly. In size, the Toulouse generally
are the largest, although sometimes equalled by the Embden. The prize Toulouse geese at the Birmingham show
weighed as high as 60 pounds per pair, and goslings forty
eight and a half pounds. This is counted the heaviest
weight ever attained. They mature early, are very hardy,
and produce an abundance of feathers.

EMBDEN, or BREMEN GEESE are of a pure white plumage, with dark flesh-colored bills, orange legs and bright
blue eyes. They should be very tall and of erect carriage,
with large square bodies. Mr. J. K. Fowler gives the
following weights of his prize geese:—the gander, (three
years old,) weighed just thirty-two and a half pounds
and his mate (a goose of the same age) pulled down
very nearly twenty-six pounds; the goslings weighed

twenty-seven and a half pounds, and twenty-four pounds. They are kept and bred largely in Saxony, and are celebrated for the delicacy of their meat. They are good layers and easily raised. The feathers, (a very important "crop" of geese are bred in quantities,) are more valuable than those of the Toulouse or any other grey geese.

THE CHINA OR HONG KONG GEESE are not so large but are unusually prolific layers. The goose will lay as many as thirty eggs before offering to sit, and will lay three or even four litters in a season. Their flesh is very superior, they mature early, are easily raised, and are readily fattened. Their eggs are not as large by about one third as the two preceding breeds, but the greatly increased quantity more than compensates. They are, besides, very ornamental, having a large protuberance at the base of the bill, and they should receive more attention from poultry breeders. In color they are both brown (like the Toulouse,) and pure snowy white. In concluding our remarks on Geese, we would strongly urge breeders and farmers everywhere to pay more attention to the breeding of this valued domestic fowl. We are glad to notice a good demand for thoroughbred geese, and trust that breeders will soon perceive the value of paying these fowls the attention they so well deserve.

RAISING DUCKS.

Farmers generally neglect the breeding of Ducks from an idea that they "eat their heads off." There is no farm poultry, if well managed, more profitable. It has been proved by actual trial that ducks often lay more eggs than hens. Their eggs, besides being much larger, and more valuable, also contain less waste. Ducks, if marketed at the right season, always bring good prices. They can be raised very easily. The eggs can be set under hens, and as many as forty or fifty young ducklings can be mothered by one hen. They require much the same feed as fowls, and if intended for the market should be liberally fed. In Aylesbury, England, where thousands of ducks are marketed every week, it is estimated that the cost of producing a couple of ducklings of nearly four pounds weight at eight weeks old is two shillings each. They fetch in the London market, during March, seventeen to nineteen shillings a couple. One great point in their favor is that they are remarkably exempt from the ravages of fatal diseases that so often depopulate a barnyard of fowls. Ducks will almost earn their living by the vast quantities of grubs and insects they destroy. Two or three ducks can be given to one drake.

The Pekin Duck, although only introduced from China in 1873, has already acquired great fame. They are by far the largest ducks in appearance, but like all Asiatic Fowls are not so large as they look, having a loose, fluffy plumage. Although sometimes equalled in weight by the Rouens, yet, as a rule, we believe they are the heaviest. They mature very early, and are excellent layers. Last

year, one duck produced 108 eggs, which were sold for
sitting, and after we were done shipping the eggs she
was not done supplying them. That was a profitable
duck, producing 108 eggs at $4.00 per dozen. Pekins
can be raised successfully with only sufficient water for
drinking; they can be confined by a very low fence, and
are very domestic. There is one drawback to them, with
which we have had some trouble. We have found that
some males fail to impregnate the eggs. This, we have
reason to think, is owing to their broad clumsy bodies.
They are clad in a beautiful coat of creamy whiteness,
with yellow bills and orange legs. A single duck has
been known to lay 200 eggs in one season. For breeding
for sale, as a fancy fowl, Pekin Ducks are undoubtedly
in great demand, and at the most satisfactory prices.
For the first year or two the ducks sold for $20 per pair,
and eggs $10 per dozen, and were eagerly sought at these
figures. But now, from the increase of the stock, they
can be had at half these prices.

AYLESBURY DUCKS are snowy white in plumage with
flesh colored bills and orange legs. They are long and
graceful in shape of body and comely in appearance. They
are especially celebrated as prolific layers; they will
commence in March and continue till June or July. They
mature early, are very hardy and easily raised. Extra
specimens have attained the extreme weights of 18 and
19 pounds per pair, but 12 to 15 pounds are good weights.
These are the ducks that are so celebrated in England
and raised in such immense quantities in the district from
which they derive their name. An Aylesbury drake
will make a very marked improvement if crossed on the
common stock.

ROUEN DUCKS are without a rival in beauty and
elegance of plumage. They resemble the wild mallards.

Choice strains are very large. There are many degenerated specimens of this variety in the country that are of
small size. They mature early and are excellent table
fowls. While not as prolific as the Aylesbury, we have
known them to lay very well, laying in the fall as well
as the spring. Their eggs are not so large as the Aylesbury.

CAYUGA DUCKS are of American origin, and are of one
solid metallic black plumage throughout. They are of
large size, good layers, and easily raised.

MUSCOVY DUCKS. These are very odd. They are dis-
tinctly a "dry land" duck, and never quack. The drakes
are the largest of all, but the ducks are rather small. They
are five weeks hatching. They are both pure white and
white and black splashed. Drakes will weigh ten and
twelve pounds each. The mules between this breed and
the water ducks make a very good table fowl, celebrated
for early maturity.

CRESTED WHITE DUCKS are very attractive. They are
pure white, with large top knots. They are of good size,
mature early, and lay well.

CALL DUCKS are small and chiefly esteemed as ornamental water fowls. They are both brown and white in
plumage, the former resembling the wild mallards.

GUINEA FOWLS.

Guineas lay a large number of eggs, which are of a very rich flavor. Their flesh is very choice and game-like. They have, however, their drawbacks, which are their inherent nature of cruelty to other poultry, and also their great propensity to wander away from home. Both these objections to them can, however, to a great degree, be overcome; the former by kind and goodly treatment of them; the latter, by furnishing secluded nests, and also not disturbing them. If a guinea hen's nest is robbed of a number of eggs at once, she will forsake it and seek a more secluded one. Hence the eggs should be gathered every day, one egg being left in the nest. They do not generally sit until late. For this reason, and also because the young guineas will be more domestic, the eggs should be set under hens. The young chicks have very small crops, and hence must have them filled very frequently, with the same food as recommended for chicks. In a natural state, guineas mate in pairs, but under domestication, one male will readily serve a couple of hens. It is very difficult to distinguish the sexes. This can be done by watching their actions, by the hen's peculiar cry, and also from the fact that the cock is more cruel to other fowls. Guineas will generally roost in the trees around their home, and are the best of " watch dogs," giving ample notice of the approach of any person in the neighborhood. The ordinary Pearl Guinea Fowl (so called from the resemblance of the spots to pearls,) are very uniformly marked with white spots in a ground color of grey purple. Most of the common guineas have patches of white, or white feathers in the wings, and are not nearly so pretty. Pure white guineas are rather rare, and are very attractive ornaments on a green lawn.

VARIETIES OF FOWLS.

BRAHMAS.—No breed of pure bred poultry, from the days of the hen fever to the present, have so universally maintained a front rank in the estimation of all poultry men, as the Brahma. They are quiet in their disposition, and very tame. Our late lamented dark Brahma cock, "Joe Hooker," was as affectionate and knowing almost as a dog. He would come into the kitchen at meal times and would quietly walk around and eat out of the hand what was given him, but never would he eat anything within his reach that was not set aside for him. Brahmas can easily be picked up anywhere by a child. A three foot fence will confine them, and no breed in the world is so well adapted to close confinement. They thrive well in the smallest quarters. They are excellent winter layers, their eggs are of varied shades. That *pure* Brahmas should lay eggs of one uniform color is an exploded bubble. They are very much inclined to sit, and this is a great drawback. They do not mature early, and are not so desirable for market pure bred as when crossed. For mothers they are the very best, when not too heavy. They have plenty of loose fluff, and will cover a goodly number of eggs. They should be of large size, but no giants. The days of the "long legged Shanghaes that could eat off the top of a barrel, and all there is in it," is past. Farmers and poulterers are beginning to realize that utility of form must be studied. It needs no demonstration to prove that it is highly unprofitable to feed corn and wheat to produce such unpalatable parts as neck and leg. Matured cocks of 12 pounds, and hens of 8 to

10 pounds, are fully as large as can generally be had in connection with other meritorious points. One peculiarity of this breed is the pea comb, which, being so small is safe against the winter's frosts.

LIGHT BRAHMAS with us are perhaps more generally bred throughout the entire country than any other breed, and yet there is always a very lively demand for good stock at satisfactory prices. They are often inclined to be long legged; this must be guarded against by judicious selection. In mating, the cock and hens should not both have dark hackles, or the progeny will be very unsatisfactory. There is a prejudice in the minds of some that Light Brahmas are delicate, on account of their plumage. This is entirely a mistake. They are altogether a most worthy breed, and invaluable to increase the size, laying and early maturity of a lot of "dunghills."

DARK BRAHMAS have nearly the same characteristics as the light. They are, however, deeper and more compact in body, with shorter legs. They are like the lights, well feathered down to the ends of the toes, but should be free from vulture hock. They are very hard to breed to the "standard," only four or five birds out of every 100 will be meritorious show birds, even from the best stock. But all the remaining birds are by no means disqualified. Many of them are generally as good, and some even better for breeding.

COCHINS are large noble looking fowls, with an abundance of loose fluffy feathers, especially in the hens, thus making them the very best mothers. Mature cocks should weigh 10 to 13 pounds, and hens 8 to 10 pounds; small weights should not be tolerated, neither should extra heavy birds be bred, if, as is generally the case, they are correspondingly badly proportioned. The legs should be abundantly feathered to the toes, but not "vulture hock-

ed." They are very docile, can be picked up by a child,
and are easily confined. They are rather poor foragers,
and must be fed liberally. They are good winter layers.
Their eggs are of various shades. They are very much
inclined to sit, and hard to break. On account of their
large size they are invaluable for crossing, whereby they
can be improved in early maturity and flesh. They have
single erect combs of fine texture. Recently a strain of
Pea Comb Partridge Cochins has been introduced, and it
is claimed for them the undoubted advantage for cold
winters. We fear, however, that should this variety become popular, the distinct types of Brahmas and Cochins
would be lost—merged into one common mixture. Cochins have so long been bred almost exclusively for large
size and fashionable form and markings, that the economic qualities have been neglected. Much can be done in
the way of improving their laying, &c. The varieties are
the BUFF, PARTRIDGE, BLACK and WHITE COCHINS. There
is also a new breed styled the Sebright Cochins not yet
recognized in the standard, nor will that name be allowed.
BUFF COCHINS are fowls of unusual beauty. They should
be of one clear buff color throughout, free from any white
or colored feathers or uneven shading. PARTRIDGE Co-
CHINS are very aristocratic, with the deep black breast
and beautifully resplendent and varied plumage of the
cock, and the exquisitely pencilled hen. For small city
yards, a more pleasing breed could scarcely be desired.
BLACK COCHINS are only recently established, and are still
subject to brassy or white feathers. They cannot fail,
however, soon to take a prominent position among their
fellows. WHITE COCHINS being of a pure snowy whiteness throughout, do not present the difficulties to the
young breeder, which are sure to be experienced in raising
the other varieties of Cochins. All Cochins possess the

same prominent characteristics and the amateur should select the variety best suited to his fancy.

Leghorns.

Of late years, Leghorns have attained a wonderful, almost miraculous popularity. And well deserved it is too. They are without doubt the best layers. They are non-sitters, although, as in all non-sitting varieties, a hen will occasionally take a notion towards incubation and will often perform her unaccustomed duties very satisfactorily. Leghorns lay as many as 200 and even 250 eggs per year. The pullets begin to lay at $4\frac{1}{2}$ and 5 months. The cockerels will crow at seven weeks old, and a very amusing sight it is to see a large flock of chicks at this age. They very soon learn to run after the hens. From the very eggs, almost before "their mother knows they are out," they are the liveliest of all chicks. They are splendid foragers, and after eight weeks old they generally pick up all their own feed, among the wheat stubble, around the barn, etc. The eggs are pure white, rather thin shell, and nearly transparent. They are not a large breed, but where eggs are desired are all the more profitable on that account, i. e., with less machinery to feed, they will shell out larger results than any other breed. The cocks weigh $4\frac{1}{2}$ to 6 pounds, and the hens $3\frac{1}{2}$ to 4 pounds. They are very hardy and easily raised. For market, although not large, they are very presentable, with bright yellow legs and skin. They have high single combs, and in this climate they are apt to get frozen in winter. This spoils their looks, but does not hurt their breeding qualities. No breed will so improve the laying qualities of barn yard fowls as Pure Leghorns.

White Leghorns were the first introduced, and are the most generally disseminated. They should be pure snowy white throughout, and entirely free from any colored feathers, or a shade of yellow. Their ear lobes should be solid white or creamy white, and in this particular good strains breed remarkably true. Their combs should be of medium size, perfectly erect and evenly formed, deeply serrated, with five prominent points, wattles pendant. Legs bright yellow. Carriage proud and upright.

Brown Leghorns are of recent introduction, but already are the most popular. They are very beautiful, resembling the Black Red Games in plumage, and from the fighting qualities of this breed, we have reason to believe they contain some game blood. We well remember our first experience with them. We had three favorite cocks, two of which were placed on one farm until one should be mated to another lot of hens. No sooner had they escaped from their respective cages than a terrible fight ensued, and before they could be separated one was killed. The Brown Leghorns are shorter in the legs and rather heavier bodied than the whites. They have bright yellow legs and skin, and are very palatable as table fowls. They are excelled by none as layers. One hen owned by a friend who kept a careful record, in ten consecutive months of last year, (including February, when she was rather " under the weather," which by-the-bye was very severe, and only laid ten eggs,) laid 223 eggs. This hen was not selected, but was the only one the party owned of this breed. The following is the record :

1st month, 23 ; 2d mo. 8 ; 3d mo. 22 ; 4th mo. 28 ; 5th mo. 27 ; 6th mo. 26 ; 7th mo. 24 ; 8th mo. 24 ; 9th mo· 24 ; 10th mo. 18 ; total, 223.

In England, this breed is becoming very popular, although as yet quite rare. They are prominently an Ame-

BROWN LEGHORNS,

WINNERS OF CENTENNIAL MEDALS.

Owned by Benson & Burpee.   Bred by W. Atlee Burpee.

rican breed. We have exported them ourselves to England, as have also other breeders. L. Wright, in his English Book of Poultry, says, "We consider them *the best layers we have ever met with.*" They have always been our own favorites, and wherever introduced they soon take the lead for eggs, both on account of immense quantity and admirable quality of same. They have all the desirable qualities of this breed to a pre-eminent degree. We give below a letter just received from a good breeder of this variety, which demonstrates an important fact.

" I will write you a word about the standard as now given for Brown Leghorns. There is here just one fault, a solid white ear lobe, and the plumage (standard) of this variety cannot consistently go together without white feathers being made allowable or dark legs not a disqualification, but *white* ear lobes—*spotless white*—and yellow legs, cannot be made to breed; it is altogether *inconsistent with natural laws.*

" In a certain number of the Poultry World, there appeared an article in which the writer stated that the original jungle fowls were nearly of the plumage of the Brown Leghorns, and some have willow legs, and some white ear lobes, to prove, doubtless that it was natural to have this white lobe. I enquired in the succeeding number of the Poultry World whether it was the yellow and dark leg birds that had the white ear lobes, but have never learned; there is too much trying to cover up the defects of the standard as given to Brown Leghorns, the most open confession I have ever seen is an article in January (22) number.

I am now running a strain of Brown Leghorns, direct descendants of the W. F. B. S. crossed on natives, and find stamina much improved, and when I get them where I can rely on them, which I know will be in 78, I will have a strain of Brown Leghorns that will not lose tail feathers in summer, nor give dark legs, but a type just to my own liking. I want lobes one-third surface white, no more. But by all means, Brother Burpee, insert in your book an open remonstrance against the wholesale slaughter of valuable points and desirable qualities, just to cater to the wants of a few fanciers like ——, who had so much to do in compiling the standard that he got in what has just ruined him, and I am glad of it. Last year, '75, in August or September, he had not 25 hens or cocks but were disqualified, on account of white feathers. I know this to be true, and am heartily glad of it."

The writer of the above is only too true to his statements. Much has been done to injure the fair fame of the Brown Leghorns by advertising solid white ear lobes and sending out birds with nearly red lobes. Raising, as we do, hundreds of Brown Leghorns, from the most carefully mated stock, we every year raise birds that are throughout free from any white tinge, with bright yellow legs and solid white lobes, but they are scarce. We consider the Brown Leghorns as difficult a breed, to handle with a view to exhibition purposes, as the Dark Brahmas, and requiring equally as much skill. Hens with pure white ear lobes are easily produced from good strains. The trouble is with the cocks. If the majority of the cocks have ear lobes two-thirds white and about five per cent pure white, with no corresponding defects, it is as good as can be expected at present. "Truth will out." Even if by letting it out we may tread on some tender toes, yet it is our only true plan in writing for the poultry public. We regard the Brown Leghorns as too valuable a breed to be altered by crossing, or to be ruined in stamina and important excellencies by a mad rush after white ear lobes, "regardless of cost." In mating, always keep in view the one great quality that endears this breed to the people—the eggs.

BLACK LEGHORNS. These are solid black in plumage, with pure white ear lobes and erect combs. They, like all black fowls, usually have dark legs. They are the smallest of the Leghorns, and although good layers, are no better than the others. They look too much like degenerated black Spanish, and it is our opinion that unless improved they will soon sink into oblivion as a variety not worthy of distinct cultivation.

DOMINIQUE LEGHORNS. These fowls are certainly very pretty, being of the uniform Dominique color, contrasting nicely with white ear lobes. The finest fowls we raised the past season, and exhibited at the Centennial, were perfect as regards Leghorn characteristics and color, but had a few black spots over the yellow legs. We have had birds of this breed with pure yellow legs, but they were faulty in the ear lobes. This variety can never compete in popularity with the Brown and White Leghorns. Some breeders claim that they are the largest of all Leghorns, and we have purchased birds of such stock which were very large—too large for pure Leghorns, and plainly showing a cross, also having nearly or quite red ear lobes.

BLACK SPANISH.

The White Face Black Spanish are one of the oldest pure breeds. They are everlasting layers of very large eggs, of excellent flavor. The yelk of the egg is not larger than ordinary eggs, the white or albumen predominating. They are very hardy if properly bred, the only danger being their large erect single combs, which will become frozen in very severe weather. They are very high in body, with fine stylish carriage. Their legs are of a lead color, becoming lighter with age. Breeding in-and-in also produces pale legs, and then a cross should be made with a very bluish-black legged cock of fresh blood. Their white face and long serrated comb extending out almost to the end of the bill are well depicted in the accompanying cut. They are very poor table fowls, but their fine eggs entitle them to a high rank among the breeds of domestic poultry.

Hamburgs.

Hamburgs are a very popular breed of non-sitting fowls. They are unrivalled in variety and beauty of plumage. Our colored frontispiece (prepared expressly for The Poultry Yard,) well represents an imported trio of the Black Hamburgs, bred by the Rev. W. Sergeatson, the most celebrated English exhibitor of this variety.

All Hamburgs possess the same general characteristics. Stylish and active in carriage, slender, rather short, blue or slaty blue legs, with deep red rose combs and close fitting pure white ear lobes. They require free range, and are then easily kept, as they are excellent foragers. They will lay upwards of 200 eggs in a year. While their eggs are not so large as those of the Leghorns, yet, as long as eggs are sold by the dozen, this makes little material difference in supplying the market. Mr. A. Beldon says of their early maturity, he has found that pullets of the pencilled varieties lay at five months; the spangled not quite so early. The varieties of Hamburgs are the silver and golden pencilled, the spangled and the solid black. The Blacks are the largest of all, and lay the largest eggs. They are also considered the most hardy. A great fault with many Black Hamburgs is a tendency to white on the face. This should never be tolerated. The face must be one rich deep red, like the wattles, contrasting strikingly with the pure white ear lobes. We have also seen fowls awarded a premium as Black Hamburgs that showed very plainly the carriage and form of the Black Spanish.

GAMES.

Games are generally familiar to everyone, and are by many considered *the* fowls. Even those who rightly disapprove of the pit and its uses, admire a really *Dead Game* Cock. No breed can equal them in true symmetry, elegance and style, with fearless expression. They are light feathered and all muscle. A game fowl will weigh much heavier than it appears. Cocks of good size will weigh 6½ pounds, and hens 5 to 5½ pounds. Their flesh is unsurpassed, being the finest flavored of any breed of fowls. They are excellent layers of fine rich eggs, much esteemed. The hens are the very best mothers and will faithfully protect their young broods. They are easily reared and are undoubtedly a very profitable breed for economic purposes—the only drawback for domestic use being their fighting qualities. But these latter adding so to their beauty and elegance, besides the extra quality of their flesh, surely warrant a little extra trouble with the young stags. When the young stags are troublesome in fighting each other, they can be penned in small coops arranged in tiers, and each one left out occasionally in a small yard, to exercise. There is always a lively demand for pure games, of fine strains at very satisfactory prices, and they are consequently one of the most profitable fancy breeds. The varieties of Games are numerous, and our limited space does not permit a description of each. The most prominent are the Black-Breasted Red, Brown-Breasted Red, Duckwings, Derby, Piles, Sumatra, White and Henny Games.

POLISH.

The Polish Fowls belong to the non-sitting breeds, and are excellent layers. Their flesh is very fine, tender and juicy. They are reasonably hardy, if kept free from wet and dampness, which they can not stand. They bear confinement well, better than any others of the laying breeds, and can be bred successfully in very small quarters. They are very tame. As an ornamental fowl, they

are *ne plus ultra*, and, combining as they do so many good qualities are excellent for a gentleman's park, while for farm use they cannot equal the Leghorns. The general form and markings are well depicted in the accompanying cut of a Bearded Golden Polish hen, the property of Messrs. C. D. Cartwright and Co. The varieties of Polish are the White-Crested Black, pure White, Golden, Silver; the three latter being both plain and bearded.

HOUDANS.

Houdans, with their fine well-formed bodies, covered with a beautiful plumage of black and white intermixed, pinky legs, and their heads almost hidden by the large crest, muffs and beards, and triple antler-like comb, and supernumary toe, cannot fail to attract attention everywhere. They are the best and most hardy of any of the French breeds, and are a fine farmer's fowl. They also bear confinement well and are easily reared. As a table fowl they are well entitled to the cognomen of "The French Dorking." They are excellent layers of fine eggs of unusually large size. The cocks are very vigorous and can serve a large number of hens. The chickens usually hatch some hours before their time, and it is a rare occurrence to find an unfertile egg. They are non-sitters. Houdans make excellent crosses on common fowls, or the Asiatics.

La Fleche and Crevecœurs are also French breeds of poultry, bred to a small extent in this country, but on account of their delicate constitutions are not valued for farmer's use. All the French breeds, it is believed, originated from a cross of the Polish and the Crevecœurs, and are in fact a Polish fowl, to all intents and purposes, but increased in size ; the same ancestry is shown by the delicate constitution which characterises nearly all the varieties."

DORKINGS.

Dorkings are of three colors or styles of markings, white, silver-grey and colored, as recognized in the American standard. But the Standard is exceedingly loose in its notice of Colored Dorkings, making no markings other than uniformity in the birds of one pen requisite. One noticeable difference between the White and Grey Dorking is that while the former must possess rose combs, square in front, firm and close fitting, terminating in a point behind; the latter are generally single combed. The Dorking is pre-eminently an English fowl—a very old variety—and true to his nature, John Bull has, in this fowl, admirably catered to his tastes. For as a table fowl, the Dorking is unsurpassed. They are indifferent, rather poor layers, but for the table they afford an extra portion of very fine meat, especially abundant in the parts most esteemed—the breast and wings. The Dorking is a heavy bodied, well put-up fowl, long broad back and close feathered. A cross with the Leghorn would make a fine fowl for farm use.

PLYMOUTH ROCKS.

Plymouth Rocks are a " made " breed of New England origin, and they are a production of which American breeders may well feel proud. No other breed of poultry combine so many excellencies nor can rival them as a " farmers' fowls." The irplumage is a plain quaker-like attire—the old-fashioned Dominique color. They have single combs and bright yellow legs. Little is sacrificed in breeding to fancy points. Their value is judged by early

maturity, large size, great utility of form and good laying
qualities. They are good sitters and excellent mothers.
They mature very early and are fit to market long before
the Asiatics. As yet they do not breed as true to feather
as some of the older established breeds, but a constant improvement is being effected.

American Dominiques.

These fowls are like the Plymouth Rocks in plumage
and bright yellow legs. But unlike the P. Rocks they
are an old-established variety, and breed very true to
color; the cocks, however, are lighter colored than the
hens. They have neat rose combs, are excellent table
fowls, good layers, free breeders, very hardy, and one of
our most valuable breeds for the general farmer. They
are not quite as large as the Plymouth Rocks.

BANTAMS.

There are several distinct breeds of Bantams; the
Games, Silver and Golden Seabrights and Black African,
being the most important. All are cultivated almost
solely as pets, and hence it is not in our province to speak
of them here. Bantams can, however, be bred in so small
a yard (five or six feet square,) that they can be kept by
many who have no better facilities. They also will produce as many eggs, although of small size, as larger fowls.
Nothing can exceed their eggs in delicacy of flavor. Small
Bantams can be run in the same yard with large Asiatics
or Plymouth Rocks, without danger of mixing.

www.ingramcontent.com/pod-product-compliance
Lightning Source LLC
Chambersburg PA
CBHW031755090426
42739CB00008B/1020